Original title:
Aloe There, Friend

Copyright © 2025 Creative Arts Management OÜ
All rights reserved.

Author: Juliette Kensington
ISBN HARDBACK: 978-1-80581-725-3
ISBN PAPERBACK: 978-1-80581-252-4
ISBN EBOOK: 978-1-80581-725-3

Touch of Nature, Ties of Friendship

In the garden, laughter grows,
With plants and pals, anything goes.
A cactus tells a joke or two,
While daisies dance in morning dew.

With each pot, a tale unwinds,
Succulent whispers in the winds.
Ferns feign elegance, try to pose,
But tumble down, oh, what a show!

The marigolds sing silly songs,
While spicy peppers tease along.
Good friends gather, drinks in hand,
And plot to outgrow this happy land.

So let's plant seeds of fun and cheer,
With roots strong enough to last year.
In every bloom, a friendship strife,
A garden party, full of life!

Nature's Gift of Whispers

In the garden, secrets sway,
Leaves giggle, come what may.
Sunshine tickles petals bright,
Nature's jokes take flight at night.

A frog croaks like a stand-up pro,
Winks at flowers, puts on a show.
Buzzing bees hum silly tunes,
As crickets dance beneath the moons.

Together in the Tenderness of Green

Two old trees share gossip bold,
Rustling leaves, their tales unfold.
Squirrels chuckle with delight,
As branches sway in moonlit night.

Underneath the sprawling boughs,
Mice play games and take their bows.
Nature's laughter fills the air,
In the green, there's joy to share.

The Resilient Heartbeat of Friendship

Cacti joke in desert hues,
"Water? Nah, we just refuse!"
A prickly laugh, a spiky grin,
True friendship thrives where few have been.

Lizards lounge on sunlit stones,
While friendly winds hum playful tones.
Every heart that beats so strong,
Knows togetherness sings a song.

Sips of Life from Nature's Cup

Raindrops laugh on thirsty ground,
Nature's sipping, oh what a sound!
Flowers bask in morning dew,
Sipping sunshine, perfect view.

Bees enjoy a nectar feast,
Cheerful buzz, to say the least.
In this cup of life, we find,
Laughter flows, joy intertwined.

Thorns and Tenderness Unite

In a patch of prickles, humor grows,
Where laughter blooms, and friendship flows.
With sharp little spikes, we jest and tease,
Yet soften the blows with giggles and ease.

Embracing the quirks of each spiky friend,
We poke fun at life, no need to pretend.
Through thick and thin, we share our glee,
A bond forged in laughter, just let it be.

A Symphony of Softness and Strength

In a garden where oddities dance and sway,
The strong and the silly have come out to play.
Together they make a hilarious tune,
With giggles that burst like flowers in June.

Rugged yet soft, a delightful blend,
With every sharp quip, they lovingly fend.
Nature's comic duo, thriving and bright,
In the spotlight of jest, they bask in delight.

Nurtured by Nature's Wisdom

In the wrinkles of wisdom, a tale unfolds,
Of playful antics and stories retold.
With spirits so light as they stretch in the sun,
These wise plants know just how to have fun.

Each crevice a cranny for tickles and giggles,
As they swap their tales with raucous wiggles.
Nature's own jesters, so witty and wise,
Sharing snickers as the sun starts to rise.

Cuddle of the Cacti

In the desert's embrace, a cuddle awaits,
With prickly hugs and soft little rates.
Through jabs and jests, we laugh and we play,
Wrapped in good humor, come what may.

A squeeze from a friend in this quirky terrain,
Where laughter's a balm for the prickly pain.
Together we thrive in our spiky delight,
A cozy confetti of joy and of light.

Healing Touch from Nature's Hand

In a pot so bright, it stands alone,
A prickly friend with a gentle tone.
When life's a mess and you feel so low,
Just give me a touch, and I'll help you grow.

Forget your worries, let laughter bloom,
With a quirky plant, there's no room for gloom.
I'll soak up your tears, just feed me some light,
Together we'll shine, oh what a delight!

The Beauty of a Silent Guardian

In a corner stands my leafy friend,
No need for words, it'll help me mend.
With tips so sharp, yet a heart so sweet,
It guards my heart like a cozy seat.

With every leaf, it whispers cheer,
A silent guardian, always near.
In the glow of the sun, we bask and sway,
Making mischief in our own green way.

Bonds Formed in Sunlit Silence

In sunlight's warmth, we find our place,
A duo in green, with style and grace.
My buddy listens; it never talks,
Just thrives beside me during walks.

With potted hugs and leafy smiles,
We share our secrets, exchanging wiles.
Our roots intertwine in joyous dance,
A quirky bond, not left to chance.

Guardians of the Indoor Oasis

In my indoor jungle, we live and play,
Guarding each other in our own fun way.
With a quirky wink, it seems to shout,
'Let's have a laugh, don't wear a pout!'

As I trip over pots and bump my knee,
It stands true, that friend looks back at me.
Through all the chaos, it stands so proud,
An odd little buddy, laughing out loud.

The Comfort of Blades and Breeze

In the garden, we thrive, so bright,
With leaves that tickle under sunlight.
We swap our jokes, not cares to send,
Just giggles shared with every bend.

A prickly hug, a laughter shard,
No need for flowers, we go hard.
Together we sway, in playful cheer,
Oh, what fun, with friends so near.

In the Arms of Verdant Company

Bound by roots, in laughter we play,
Green giants dance, by night and day.
With every rustle, a chuckle rings,
Nature's delight, the joy it brings.

Together we bask in friendship's glow,
Whispering secrets only we know.
With pot and soil, we weave our tale,
In this green world, we shall not fail.

Cactus Heartbeat

In the desert heat, we stand so bold,
A prickly bunch, with stories untold.
We share our tales of sun and rain,
And laugh out loud, drowning all pain.

Bouncing shadows in the midday sun,
Poking fun, oh, what silly fun!
With a heartbeat that's sharp, yet so sweet,
Our friendship endures, a prickly feat.

Friendship's Pulse

Hear the whispers of the green brigade,
With roots entwined, let worries fade.
A jab, a quip, no need to fret,
Our camaraderie is no regret.

Silly poses, a gentle tease,
In our leafy realm, we find our ease.
With every chuckle, our spirits rise,
Unfurling joy beneath the skies.

Serenity in Soft Green Shadows

Beneath the fronds, we chuckle low,
In shaded peace, our giggles flow.
With soft whispers of the breeze,
Together we share sweet memories.

The world outside, a distant hum,
In our soft green nook, we overcome.
With every mishap, a joke is born,
In this sanctuary, no heart is worn.

A Tonic of Togetherness

In a pot, we grow side by side,
With a laugh, we take life in stride.
When days get tough, just take a peek,
Our humor's strong, never meek.

We sip on jokes, like sweet, cool tea,
Our banter blooms, wild and free.
Roots intertwine, it's quite the show,
Laughter's the best way to grow!

Sunshine's warmth brings us cheer,
In our garden, there's no fear.
With each pun, our spirits lift,
Friendship's our magical gift.

Leaves of Loneliness

In the corner where shadows creep,
A tale of woe, I cannot keep.
Alone I sit, my leaves are sad,
Not a soul to share the rad.

The whispering wind says, "Don't despair!"
"Just crack a joke, show some flair!"
But all my puns just drift away,
A plant without friends can't play.

The sun shines bright upon my pot,
Yet here I sit, what a sad lot.
If only for laughs, I had a crew,
My leaves could flourish, sprout anew!

Bonding Beneath the Sun

Under the sun, we gather 'round,
Silly stories and laughs abound.
With sunscreen slathered on our skin,
We have a blast, let the fun begin!

A picnic spread, good snacks galore,
We munch and chatter, who could want more?
Like roots entangled, friends we find,
In every joke, our spirits bind.

Twisting and turning, we dance with glee,
Plant pals forever, just you and me.
As we bask in warmth, our hearts entwine,
In this sunny space, life's simply divine!

The Friendship of Photosynthesis

In the sunlight where we thrive,
Joined together, oh how we jive!
Breathing in joy, exhaling the fun,
Photosynthesis? No, it's just a pun!

With every ray that kisses our leaves,
We share our secrets, the fun never leaves.
Chlorophyll's green, but our smiles are bright,
Together we laugh, oh what a sight!

As we grow tall, and reach for the sky,
We'd high-five each other, if roots could fly.
In this garden, our bond's evergreen,
A friendship that shines, pure and keen!

The Sweetness of Sunlit Memories

In the garden, we do prance,
Sunshine grants us quite a chance.
Laughing with our leafy mates,
Watch out for the sneaky late.

Mischief blooms beneath the rays,
Frogs and bees join in our plays.
With vibrant colors all around,
Giggles echo, joy is found.

We dance lightly, toes in dirt,
Wiggling like a shirtless shirt.
From morning light till evening's rest,
Nature's joys, we feel so blessed.

Memories sweet, like sticky jam,
Laughter stirs, a living sham.
Sunlit days, forever spun,
With a wink, we greet the fun.

Harmony in a Hushed Green Space

In whispers soft, the leaves conspire,
To tickle toes as we retire.
Quiet giggles fill the air,
Who knew vines could hold such flair?

Rustling grass, a secret plea,
Squirrels tease from every tree.
Nature hums a funny song,
Join the dance, it won't be long.

A gentle breeze, a witty breeze,
Lifts our spirits with such ease.
Remember when we tried to climb?
Your slip was quite the funny crime!

Hushed green space, a joyful plot,
In every crack, there's laughter caught.
We'll chuckle 'til the stars align,
In this slice of life, we shine.

Wrapped in Nature's Caress

Nestled snug in leafy wraps,
We giggle with the furry chaps.
Butterflies in silly flight,
Making mischief, oh what a sight!

The sun peeks through with teasing rays,
Painting smiles in goofy ways.
Tickled plants sway to our tune,
As if they know we'll dance till noon.

A ladybug drops by to say,
"What's the buzz? Let's dance today!"
In this grove, our laughter blooms,
Filling cracks and empty rooms.

Surprises hide in every nook,
Nature's comic, oh what a hook!
Wrapped in joy, we simply thrive,
In this silliness, we're alive!

The Vitality of Growing Together

Hand in hand, we start to sprout,
With every laugh, we twist about.
Inch by inch, like vines we climb,
Growing stronger, oh how sublime!

Each day brings a playful tease,
Racing roots beneath the leaves.
Nature chuckles, wise and bold,
While we share our tales retold.

Through tangled paths, our laughter weaves,
Growing friendships, like autumn leaves.
One little poke from a twig's end,
Sparks a giggle that won't bend.

Life is ripe, the harvest near,
Among the plants, we shed our fear.
Together we'll stretch toward the sun,
In our garden, the jokes are spun.

Flourishing Spirits in Nature's Care

In the garden where we play,
Laughter blooms like flowers sway.
Sunshine tickles every leaf,
Nature's giggle brings relief.

Buzzing bees are our good pals,
Chasing dreams, we skip like jails.
Dancing shadows, bright and spry,
Join us under this clear sky.

Potted plants wear funny hats,
Conversing with the chubby cats.
Worms in trenches tell their tales,
While wind whispers through the bales.

So let's toast with frosty drinks,
To leafy friends and joyful kinks.
Nature's whimsy, hearts in tune,
We'll laugh together 'neath the moon.

Safe Harbor in a Garden of Thorns

Within the thorns, a shelter grows,
A prickly place where laughter flows.
With every spike, a joke is found,
Friends surround us, love renowned.

Cacti wear the silliest frowns,
Fooling about in nature's gowns.
Roses blush as laughter flows,
Together, we create the prose.

We guard our hearts, but what the hey,
Let's tickle thorns and laugh away.
In this warm, sweet, buttoned-up den,
We find the joy of silly zen.

Puns take flight on a summer's breeze,
In a garden that aims to please.
Though sometimes sharp, we're never alone,
In this harbor, we call our own.

Embracing the Wild Within

In tangled vines, we lose our way,
Yet that's the fun we love to play.
A wild dance beneath the moon,
Howling laughs like a silly tune.

Ferns wear crowns of leafy green,
Waving "hello" like a queen.
Squirrels chatter, birds take flight,
Join the party, day and night.

Funny friends with nature's flair,
We jump on roots without a care.
Planting seeds of pure delight,
In wild places, hearts take flight.

With every twist and every turn,
The wild within begins to burn.
Embrace the chaos, let it spin,
In laughter's arms, we dive right in!

Serene Moments in Leafy Company

Beneath the shade, we find our peace,
Leafy whispers say to cease.
A lazy sunbeam warms the ground,
In gentle joys, true smiles abound.

Crickets chirp a silly song,
In our circle, where we belong.
A picnic spread with snacks galore,
Moments like these, we can't ignore.

Green shadows play with twinkling lights,
Tickling toes as day turns night.
With leafy friends, we share our dreams,
In moments bright, nothing seems as it seems.

So let's gather 'neath the trees,
Telling stories carried on the breeze.
In serene company, life's delights,
We savor laughter, our hearts take flight.

The Shade of Friendship

In the garden where we meet,
Sunshine tickles our bare feet.
You're the plant that always thrives,
Sprouting joy, you keep us alive.

Your colors bright, yet so absurd,
A spiky tale, it's quite the word.
When shade is needed, I'll seek you,
For laughter blooms in friends so true.

We share a pot, though roots may tangle,
In summer heat, we'll laugh and wrangle.
With every leaf, a story grows,
In friendship's sun, our garden glows.

Growing Together Amidst Thorny Times

When life gets prickly, don't you fret,
Together we'll make the best duet.
You share your quirks, I'll add some cheer,
In this wild patch, we persevere.

We weave our tales with every sweat,
In thorny times, we won't forget.
With laughter's spice and love's great grace,
We'll bloom, my friend, in this odd place.

So when the winds of chaos blow,
We'll root each other, let it show.
Spikes and all, we still shall rise,
Two wacky plants beneath the skies.

Flourishing Beneath Dappled Light

In a corner where shadows play,
We bask in sunlight, come what may.
Your humor sprouted, oh so bright,
In dappled dreams, we take our flight.

You crack a joke, I can't contain,
With every grin, we dance in rain.
Under the leaves, we laugh and sigh,
Rooted in joy, we reach the sky.

A swirl of colors, whimsically free,
In this jungle, just you and me.
Growing wildly, we'll never part,
In nature's quilt, you steal my heart.

Embracing Imperfections in Nature

With crooked leaves and lopsided charm,
You keep me grounded, safe from harm.
Our quirks are treasures, don't you see?
In nature's mess, we're meant to be.

You're a bit wobbly, I'm a bit shy,
But together, we reach the sky.
With laughter etched in every vein,
Our colorful flaws break every chain.

Though nature's scheme may seem bizarre,
Among the weeds, you are my star.
In our imperfect garden's light,
Friendship flourishes, pure delight.

Nature's Embrace

In my pot, so lush and bright,
Sits a plant, quite a sight.
With leaves like arms, it gives a hug,
A silent friend, all snug and snug.

When I'm sad or feeling low,
It just sits there, stealing the show.
No words are shared, but still, it seems,
To sprout up joy in my wild dreams.

You talk to me with silent glee,
Growing steadfast, wild and free.
My green companion, a comical sprout,
Who knew plants could turn life about!

So here's to you, my leafy mate,
You lift my mood and lighten fate.
In your presence, I can't help but grin,
With every laugh, a new leaf spins.

Green Companion's Whisper

A friend so green, with style and flair,
In sunlight, you simply don't care.
You sip the sun, I drink my tea,
Together we thrive, a sight to see.

With spiky hair and a charming pose,
You're the coolest plant, everybody knows.
While I chat away, you nod along,
With your silent wisdom, you can't go wrong.

You absorb my worries, like a sponge,
In your company, I never plunge.
Giggling softly when things go awry,
Together we laugh, oh my, oh my!

In this garden, you reign supreme,
A quirky duo, living the dream.
With you by my side, the days are bright,
Oh, my green pal, what a funny sight!

The Healing Touch of Leaves

A miracle grows right by my chair,
Its leafy hands wave, without a care.
It patches up my occasional woes,
In the heart of my home, it always grows.

I spill my beans; you soak up the chat,
With your keen leaves and charming pat.
Who needs a doctor when I have you?
You listen well; it's true, it's true!

You sway to the rhythm of the breeze,
Turning down woes like a funky tease.
With every giggle, my spirits lift,
Your remedy comes with a funny gift.

In this leafy realm, laughter's a must,
With you around, life's never a bust.
So here's to the healing touch you bring,
In our silly world, let's dance and sing!

Succulent Solace

In my home, you sit just right,
A charming sight, a quirky light.
You puff up joy on a dreary day,
With every bump, you make me sway.

A prickly friend that's never shy,
In your company, I can't deny.
You keep it real with simple flair,
My goofy buddy, beyond compare!

You soak up sunshine, I pour the tea,
Together we share a grand ol' spree.
What's better than laughter, oh wait, you see,
This plant and I, we live carefree!

So here's to you, with your spiky grin,
A succulent life is about to begin.
With your funny charm and verdant cheer,
I'll hold you close, my friend so dear!

Nature's Hand in Healing Hearts

In the garden where laughter grows,
Green fingers dance, as friendship flows.
With a wink from the sun, it plays its part,
Nature's magic mending every heart.

Whispers in leaves, a giggling breeze,
Cracking jokes, bending trees with ease.
Like a bandage that smiles back at you,
Healing with humor, it's just what we do.

Each petal's a tickle, each thorn a jest,
Nature's our therapist, truly the best.
Giggles erupt from the soil's embrace,
As we frolic together in this joyful space.

With roots intertwined in life's silly dance,
We flourish together, given the chance.
So let's spread laughter like sunlight anew,
In this garden of joy, it's just me and you.

Blooms of Trust in a Shared Space

In a patch where daisies tell their tales,
Laughter erupts as friendship prevails.
Trust blossoms bright in the sun's warm glow,
A bond like roots, through the soil we grow.

With petals like gossip, colors so bold,
We share our secrets that never get old.
In every sprout lies a joke or two,
Sprinkling joy in the morning dew.

The bees laugh softly, joining our fun,
Buzzing around like they've just won a run.
With pollen of laughter, they spread their cheer,
In this garden of trust, we have nothing to fear.

So let's plant our dreams in this vibrant space,
Together we'll bloom, in time's warm embrace.
In the garden of giggles, where we slowly trace,
Our journey of laughter, our favorite place!

Respite Under the Watchful Eyes

Under the watch of the wise old tree,
We rest from the world, just you and me.
With branches like arms that wrap us tight,
We giggle away the warm afternoon light.

The grass tickles toes, a soft, fuzzy bed,
As we share funny stories, the giggles spread.
The squirrels roll their eyes, as if to declare,
They've heard the same tales, but we just don't care.

A gentle breeze plays with leaves overhead,
It's nature's way of nodding, 'You're well fed.'
With smiles all around, we lounge in delight,
Under the watchful eyes, everything feels right.

So here we'll sit, under this leafy abode,
Where laughter is bountiful, joy gets bestowed.
In this cozy retreat, where fun never dies,
We'll laugh together beneath nature's wise.

Outstretched Leaves and Open Hearts

With outstretched leaves, we reach for the sky,
In a dance of delight as the clouds float by.
Open hearts flutter like butterflies' wings,
Finding friendship in what every season brings.

In the shade of the branches, we share our delight,
With whispers that shimmer in the soft twilight.
Like vines we twist in this playful embrace,
Creating a sanctuary, a joyful space.

The quirky critters join in our cheer,
As we sing silly songs that only we hear.
With laughter as fertilizer, we truly thrive,
In this garden of fun, together alive.

So let's raise our leaves to the sky and sing,
Celebrating the joy that true friendship can bring.
With laughter as our sunshine, let's never depart,
In this colorful realm, with open, eager hearts.

Conversations in a Leafy Sanctuary

In the garden, whispers grow,
Plants chat softly, time moves slow.
"Did you hear the one about the seed?"
"No, but do tell, I'm all ears indeed!"

Basil jokes with fragrant thyme,
"Why do plants never commit a crime?"
"Because they always turn over a new leaf!"
"Ha! That's a funny little belief!"

Cacti poke fun at the path,
"Why's the fern always doing the math?"
"It calculates how to share the sun!"
"Oh dear, another pun has begun!"

From leaf to leaf, the laughter flies,
As the sun peeks through, and friendship ties.
In this leafy refuge, joy abounds,
With roots of humor in playful grounds.

Finding Ease in Nature's Embrace

In the meadow, laughter flows,
Bumblebees hum, while the breeze blows.
"Did you see that squirrel take a leap?"
"More like a tumble, it fell in a heap!"

The daisies dance, they can't contain,
Giggling softly as they spread their chain.
"How do flowers get fit so fast?"
"They exercise their petals, oh what a blast!"

A butterfly winks at the shade,
"You think you can find me? Don't be afraid!"
"I'm all for fun, but where's my treat?"
"A blossom snack? Now that's hard to beat!"

In nature's arms with no haste,
Every moment savored, never misplaced.
Each chuckle rings through bright and free,
In this playful world, just you and me.

Gentle Green Shadows on Sunlit Days

Under the shade, the leaves conspire,
Sharing secrets, building a fire.
"Why do the willows weep so much?"
"I bet it's the gossip and keep in touch!"

A lizard smirks as it suns its back,
"You think that critter gives a snack?"
"No, but it sure can take a holiday!"
"Well, I'd join, if I had my way!"

The mushrooms cluster, forming a band,
"Let's throw a party on this soft land!"
"But where's the cake? Or ice cream treat?"
"Under the leaves, you'll find a sweet seat!"

Beneath the green, the humor swells,
Nature's comedy, with stories it tells.
A canvas of laughter, inscribed in play,
The gentle shadows brighten our day.

Cultivating Bonds Under the Blue Sky

In the open air, the laughter blooms,
Each plant grinning, dispelling glooms.
"Why did the sprout talk to the stone?"
"It needed advice, it felt all alone!"

Sunflowers stretch with their sunny heads,
"What if a weed just wanted to spread?"
"Then we'll share tea and discuss its plight!"
"A friendly meeting, that feels just right!"

A cloud drifts by with a chuckle too,
"What's the moss doing, in all of this blue?"
"Just taking a break, it deserves a spa!"
"A mossy retreat? Ha! How bizarre!"

Under bright skies, they bond and weave,
With giggles and jokes, none want to leave.
In this garden, both funny and wise,
Friendships blossom under open skies.

Refreshing Moments with My Green Ally

In a pot you sit so stout,
I water you, you sprout.
A drip here, a splash there,
Your thirst begins to flare.

While I ponder life's great woes,
You just chill, strike a pose.
Oh, how you lean with grace,
A spiky crown on your face!

Friends come and friends will go,
But your steadfastness steals the show.
A jolly green, patient sage,
You're the star, I'm the stage!

When life gets too tough to handle,
You wave your leaves like a candle.
Here's to laughter, joy, and cheer,
With you, my friend, so near!

The Silent Assurance of Green Leaves

Peeking from a shelf so high,
You wink at me with a sigh.
I'm stressed, but you just breathe,
In your calm, worries sheathe.

Not a word, yet you advise,
With your wise, unblinking eyes.
Oh, what a leafy therapist,
In your presence, I insist!

Through the chaos of the day,
You're my shelter, come what may.
No talking back or sass,
Just leafy love in a grassy mass!

You green genius, on display,
Making life's troubles melt away.
In the quiet, we both thrive,
For in stillness, we alive!

Curves of Calm in a Chaotic World

Your curves sway with subtle flair,
While I boldly pull my hair.
In a world spinning fast and wild,
You're my unbothered, green child.

While everything's a crazy race,
You lounge in your comfy space.
With each wave of your foliage,
You simply hold your own mirage.

I rush around, a frantic bird,
Yet you hum without a word.
Oh, the irony's not so lost,
You're chilled, while I pay the cost!

So here's to you, my leafy friend,
In your presence, I'll soon mend.
Your curves, a lesson soft and wise,
In this whirlwind, I'll rise!

Matching Grows Among Gentle Giants

In a garden full of glee,
You and I wild and free.
Among the gentle giants tall,
We laugh and dance, heed the call.

You tower there, a spiky crown,
While I trip and tumble down.
Your laughter's leaves, they rustle light,
In our fun, we take flight!

We're mismatched but side by side,
In our laughs, we take pride.
With a shake of your spiky head,
You keep me safe, never dread.

In the shade of those who loom,
You offer sweet, green perfume.
Together, we'll navigate this spree,
My quirky plant, just you and me!

Resilience Wrapped in Tenderness

In a pot too small, it thrives,
With winks of green, it comes alive.
When troubles come, it does not flee,
Just gives a shrug and sips some tea.

Beneath the sun, it shares a grin,
A prickly laugh hides all within.
Its soothing touch dispels all gloom,
A gentle poke to make you bloom.

A Conservatory of Kindred Spirits

In this cozy nook, we gather round,
With leafy friends, laughter is found.
They whisper secrets, tales untold,
As we swap stories, bold and gold.

One's got jokes, a funny chap,
While another naps in sunlight's lap.
We toast with water, a silly cheer,
To growing friendships that thrive here!

Conversations Among the Leaves

Leaves chatter soft, like gossip queens,
The air is light, filled with silliness scenes.
One says it's hot, the other agrees,
While we sip on air, like sweet summer breeze.

A flower pipes up, "What's with the fuss?"
"We're all just plants, come join us!"
Laughter erupts from each little sprout,
What a joyful, green-friendly bout!

Blooms of Warmth and Kindness

In a patch of sun, we spread delight,
With giggles soft, we shine so bright.
We swap our roots, we share our shade,
In this garden, friendships are made.

Every bloom's a smile, every stem a hug,
A cozy corner, all snug as a bug.
We stand together, strong and true,
Oh, what a colorful crew!

When Thorns Blossom into Friendship

In a garden so bright, with laughter we'd play,
You poked me with thorns, said, "I'm fun this way!"
A prickly encounter, yet I couldn't resist,
Laughter and friendship, impossible to miss.

You watered my woes, we danced in the sun,
With each little jaunt, we knew we had won.
With barbs all around, we navigated cheer,
Our friendship, it blossomed, through giggles and beer.

The bees buzzed along to our whimsical tune,
With sunlight and smiles, we brightened the noon.
Sometimes we'd argue, but never for long,
In our thorny tale, we knew we belonged.

So here's to the laughs, and the pokes and the pricks,
In the chaos of life, our friendship just clicks.
When thorns turn to laughs, and blooms surprise,
A bond in the garden, that sweetens our skies.

Nature's Embrace in Times of Strife

Amidst the tall weeds, where the wild things grow,
You tripped over roots, but you stole the show!
With mud on your face, you started to laugh,
Nature's wild chaos, our silly staff.

The branches would sway, as we wobbled around,
Each tumble and blush, we both lost and found.
With nature our backdrop, we climbed and we slipped,
Through laughter we wandered, life's ultimate trip.

In storms we would dance, twirling leaves in the air,
With thunder as music, we didn't have care.
A wild wind's buffet, but we'd handle the strife,
With trees as our witnesses, we flourished in life.

So here's to nature, its giggles and spins,
In moments of chaos, that's where friendship begins.
Together we thrive, despite all of the fuss,
In nature's embrace, it's just you and us.

Tending to Life's Tender Roots

We planted our hopes in a curious pot,
With herbs on the side, and a flower—why not?
Watered by friendship, we nurtured the ground,
In this garden we've grown, we joyously found.

Through sunny days bright, and rains full of cheer,
We pruned all our worries, we conquered our fear.
With each little sprout, we'd crack jokes and laugh,
Our bond turns to nectar, as sweet as a half.

We'll grow like the vines that can't help but entwine,
With roots deep and strong, our future will shine.
So here's to the blooms, both tender and spry,
In tending to roots, friendship reaches the sky.

With potting soil stories, and sunlight so warm,
Together we flourish, amidst any storm.
Through laughter and gardening, nurturing vibes,
We blossom through life, as our heart's joy imbibes.

Heartbeats Amongst the Greenery

In a jungle of green, where we giggle and sway,
You startled a frog, it hopped far away!
With chuckles and gasps, we made quite the sounds,
Heartbeats through leaves, as joy knows no bounds.

Amidst vibrant ferns, we created a game,
Who spots the odd bug? Oh, what fun! Who's to blame?
With smiles like sunshine, and spirits that soar,
In this leafy wonder, we always want more.

The rustle of branches sang sweet songs of rhyme,
With laughter, we measured such blissful time.
Heartbeats echoed softly, as we ran wild and free,
In nature's embrace, just you and me.

So here's to the fun, and the laughter we share,
In this vibrant greenery, without a care.
Together we revel, as life spins its play,
With hearts intertwined, forever we'll stay.

Harmonious Growth in Sunny Corners

In pots we gather, side by side,
Our roots entangled, we laugh with pride.
You sneak my water; I steal your sun,
But together we're sprouting, oh what fun!

With leaves like arms raised to the sky,
We bask in warmth, oh me, oh my!
A little bit quirk, a whole lot of green,
In our happy patch, we reign supreme!

When clouds roll in and shadows creep,
We tell the tales of soil so deep.
With wit so sharp as our thorns, we jest,
Among the sunny corners, we feel blessed!

Laughter echoes through the garden's frame,
We've tangled our roots, it's a fun little game.
In nature's embrace, we thrive and cheer,
Oh, what a joy, with friends so dear!

Care Amongst the Green Guardians

In the bustling patch of leafy friends,
We lend our care, it never ends.
You take my shade, I share your breeze,
Together we bloom with graceful ease!

With a wink and a nod, we swap our leaves,
Planting joy in the plots, as nature believes.
While squirrels may dance, and bees may hum,
We chuckle at critters, oh, such fun!

You tickle my roots, and I poke your stem,
Under the sun, we toss whimsy's gem.
With mud on our faces and smiles so wide,
In the green guardians, we take great pride!

We whisper secrets, we concoct our schemes,
In the dance of growth, our friendship beams.
With laughter galore, and joy to spare,
Such care amongst us, beyond compare!

A Tapestry of Companionable Leaves

Together we weave a tapestry bright,
With vines intertwined, a beautiful sight.
Your shade keeps me cool, my blooms catch the eye,
In our green corner, we reach for the sky!

A rustle of laughter as wind breezes by,
We play peek-a-boo, oh my, oh my!
With each gentle sway, we dance in the air,
In this leafy chorus, we weave without care!

You share your sunlight; I share my cheer,
Our roots tell stories, each one sincere.
A twist here, a turn there, we grow with a grin,
In this well-tended space, we flourish within!

When water drops fall like giggles in play,
We soak in the joy, come what may.
In vibrant hues, our friendship is bold,
A tapestry rich, worth more than gold!

The Inner Light of Verdant Friends

In shady groves where laughter sings,
We sprout our giggles and share the bling.
Your humor's like sunshine, warm and bright,
In our leafy realm, we bask in delight!

As whispers of breeze tickle our leaves,
We jest of petals, and tease of thieves.
Oh, how you wiggle when the sun shines right,
Our little shenanigans bring such light!

With roots running deep, we anchor our jest,
Planting seeds of joy, we venture the best.
Though storms may come and winds may blow,
Our inner light glows, putting on a show!

In the garden of laughter, we bloom every day,
With friends so dear, in a funny display.
We team up in growth with love and cheer,
In this verdant wonder, we hold each other near!

Companionship of the Green

In the corner, you sit so still,
Your pot's a throne, just like a hill.
I spill my secrets, you soak them in,
With your prickly laugh, where do I begin?

My friends all laugh, think you're a joke,
But you give me shade with every poke.
When I trip and fall, you're there to cheer,
Your succulent smile wipes away the fear.

Whispers of wisdom, you softly parade,
In this wild jungle, you make the grade.
While I'm human, tangled in fate,
You just grow strong, and I feel great.

So here's to you, my leafy mate,
In this friendship, there's no debate.
With laughter and green, we conquer the day,
In our silly bond, we'll forever stay.

Nature's Loyal Confidant

In this garden, you're quite the ace,
With your sharp wit, you keep up the pace.
Tales of the sun and soft summer breeze,
You listen to all, with remarkable ease.

While others complain, you just sit and grin,
How do you do it? Where do I begin?
Your silent wisdom, always on cue,
Makes all my worries feel like they'll stew.

With your prickly charm and vibrant hues,
You brighten my mornings with all kinds of views.
Oh, how I wish cars could really fly,
So we could road trip—just you and I.

Cheers to you, my loyal green sage,
Together we dance through every age.
Your quirks, they match my clumsy style,
A friendship so odd, it makes life worthwhile.

The Quiet Strength of Leafy Friends

In a world of chatter, you quietly grow,
No need for drama, just let it flow.
With your leaves so strong, you stand so proud,
In our little realm, we've gathered a crowd.

You soak up my blunders like morning dew,
While I spill laughter, never turning blue.
When the days get tough, I can always depend,
On your gentle spirit, my leafy friend.

Your prickles may poke, but your heart is gold,
In the game of life, you never fold.
A bond so unique, like tea with a twist,
How could I forget you? You've been missed!

So let's toast our roots, in this joyful spree,
With you by my side, how fun it will be!
In this garden of giggles, forever we'll dwell,
With laughs and good vibes, oh, I can tell!

Cultivating Kindred Spirits

In a pot so snug, you stand in place,
With your leafy grin, you light up the space.
We trade our jokes like seeds in the air,
Growing our laughter without a care.

While others rush past, you take it slow,
A wise old soul with tales to bestow.
Through rainy days and sunny cheer,
You're the one I want to keep near.

Your green little fingers wave as I share,
Awkward stories that hang in the air.
Through thick and thin, you listen with glee,
A steadfast buddy, just you and me.

So, here's to our antics, both strange and bright,
In the garden of friendship, you feel just right.
With a sprinkle of laughter, we thrive and grow,
In this quirky bond, let good times flow!

Whispered Secrets in a Leaf

In a garden green, I peep,
A spiky friend that's quite the leap.
With secrets whispered in its spine,
It jokes about the sun's design.

It beams with pride, my leafy mate,
Chuckling at the sun's debate.
"It's not so hot," it teases me,
"Just basking here, so wild and free!"

Each morning brings new laughs and cheer,
When back to life, the leaves appear.
With every cut, it winks and glows,
"Don't fret, my friend, it's how life goes!"

So here we stand, my prickly pal,
Under sun's watch, we laugh and gal.
In whispers shared, we thrive and jest,
With nature's laughter, we're truly blessed!

Together in the Desert Sun

Underneath the blazing light,
Two odd friends share quite a sight.
One's tall and green, the other flat,
They share the shade and giggle a chat.

"Do you feel that?" the flat one quips,
"It's the heat, making your spine flips!"
The green one nods with spiky flair,
"It's just my way to have some air!"

In a world of sand and sunlit beams,
They make a pair of silly schemes.
Chasing lizards, dodging bees,
Who knew they'd laugh with such great ease?

So hand in leaf, they share a plight,
Together they shine, stars in their light.
In the desert dance, they'll never run,
For laughter blooms in the scorching fun!

Nature's Healer by My Side

Next to me, my healer stands,
With spiky arms and sunny plans.
It winks at cuts and scrapes I see,
"Don't worry, mate, just trust in me!"

With a twist and turn, it takes a stance,
In every bruise, it starts to dance.
"Apply some goo, you'll feel brand new,
It's just my magic, tried and true!"

Friends with benefits, as we both say,
Healing's just a leaf away.
Together we laugh through thick and thin,
With a green friend, you always win!

So here's to joy, and healing, too,
With a spiky buddy, life's brighter hue.
In laughter's glow, we take a ride,
Nature's healer, always by my side!

A Journey Through Prickly Paths

On a journey through the thorny maze,
My spiky friend and I share grins ablaze.
With each step, we find new laughs,
In prickly hugs and gentle gaffes.

"Watch your step!" it shouts with glee,
"Here's a path just for you and me!"
It nudges me into a quirky spot,
"Can't have an adventure without getting caught!"

Through laughter we wiggle, turn and sway,
On prickly paths, we find our way.
Nothing can stop our silly quest,
In this leafy world, we're truly blessed!

So onward we go, through thick and thin,
With giggles echoing, we always win.
In every twist, we find the fun,
A journey shared, under the sun!

The Gentle Shield in the Warmth

Oh, look at you, standing tall,
With your spikes and your charm — not small.
You shield me from the sun's hot glow,
A leafy friend, always in the flow.

With laughter, we sip the day's sweet sun,
In a pot or a garden, we're having fun.
Your prickles can in fact surprise,
But your heart is soft, oh how it sighs.

My spiky buddy in the heat,
Giving shade with your comfy seat.
You make life a little less bland,
Oh, gentle shield, I raise my hand!

Together we dance in breezy air,
Who thought a plant could show such flair?
In antics and giggles, we'll remain,
A bond unbroken, through sun and rain.

Comfort Found in a Spiky Embrace

In the realm of green, you shine bright,
With your pointy tips, oh what a sight!
You beckon me with your leafy grin,
A quirky hug where laughs begin.

Your spikes might seem a little rough,
But we both know you've got the stuff.
Underneath that spiky facade,
Lies a heart so big, it's just not odd.

We sip on sunshine, share a smile,
In this garden, we've walked a mile.
What a joy to bask and share,
Spiky embrace? Who would care?

Let's prance around this silly space,
In the warm glow, we'll find our place.
You're my sidekick, despite your frame,
Together, we'll always share the same.

A Garden of Quiet Camaraderie

In this oasis of green delight,
You're my buddy, my shimm'ring light.
With curls and swirls, you stand so near,
A friendship grown with every cheer.

Amongst the petals, we find our way,
With whispers of fun, we dance and play.
Your prickles tease, but I don't mind,
In this garden, true joy we find.

We chuckle through the gentle breeze,
Sharing moments that aim to please.
A quirk here, a twist there,
With you, my friend, life's full of flair.

So let's grow together, side by side,
In this realm where all can abide.
Sweet laughter blooms, and worries cease,
In our garden, we find our peace.

Roots Tied in Earth and Kindness

Digging deep, our roots entwined,
With every laugh, more love defined.
Though you're spiky, I don't mind,
In the soil of life, we're both aligned.

Oh, the chats we have each day,
In sunlit moments, come what may.
Your humor sharp, but heart so kind,
With every quirk, our lives intertwined.

In the warmth of light, we make our home,
In this patch of earth, we freely roam.
Together we weather every storm,
With a prickly friend, life is warm.

So here's to laughter and days so bright,
With you beside me, all feels right.
A friendship bloom, so wild and free,
In this earthy bond, just you and me.

A Gentle Leaf's Greeting

Hello there, oh prickly mate,
How's your sun? Isn't it great?
Soak it up, don't be shy,
Just a leaf, giving a try.

Bask in the warm, golden rays,
Counting each and every phase.
Twisting and turning, what a sight,
You dance in the breeze, feeling light.

Whispers float on golden air,
Plant gossip that goes everywhere.
Did you hear the news today?
Another pot is on its way!

Shadows cool us, friends so dear,
No need for worry; no need for fear.
In this garden, we'll always blend,
Growing together, to the very end.

Cacti Conversations

Hey, pointy pal, how's the vibe?
Sharp as always, ready to jibe.
You could use a touch of chill,
But I see you've got quite the will.

Sipping sun, with a glass of dew,
What's the latest joke in your crew?
I hear succulents are on a roll,
Those smooth-talking greens take the toll.

Can't help but laugh; they prance so bright,
With their plump leaves, such a sight!
While we sit here, tough as nails,
Trading quips on the wind-tossed trails.

Oh, but don't forget, you're my star,
Even with spines, you're never too far.
Cacti unite, through thick and thin,
In this desert, let the fun begin!

The Comfort of Verdant Friends

In the pot with a splashy grin,
Green companions, let fun begin.
Sharing sunlight, our joyful pact,
Growing together, that's a fact!

Oh leafy friend, with roots so deep,
You and I, we'll never sleep.
Chasing shadows, basking bright,
A sprinkle of joy, what a delight!

When storms come, we stand so tall,
Through thick and thin, we've seen it all.
Sprouts of laughter in misty spray,
Dancing droplets make our day!

In this garden, hugs abound,
Verdant pals, joy is found.
We bloom and cheer, with hearts in tune,
Together we'll laugh, morning to noon!

Herbal Hugs and Sunny Days

Beneath the sun, a herbal cheer,
With warm hugs, I hold you near.
Cuddle close, oh fuzzy mate,
In this garden, life is great!

You twirl so soft in gentle light,
What's the gossip? Everything's bright!
A sprinkle here, a spray there,
We share secrets in fragrant air.

The bees buzz loud with tales to tell,
Of all the blooms they've loved so well.
With each petal, comes silly rhymes,
Laughter grows in cheerful climes.

So let's embrace this sunny haze,
With herbal hugs on brightening days.
Together we'll thrive, side by side,
In this green world, we take our ride!

Cherished Nature's Allies

In gardens where the sun does gleam,
Lives a plant with quite the dream.
Spikes like armor, yet so sweet,
With gel so cool it can't be beat.

It whispers tales of healing balm,
While perched on shelves, so cool and calm.
A best friend for your skin's delight,
In every shade, a charming sight.

When summer's sun starts to blaze,
This green pal knows just the ways.
With laughter, we apply and smirk,
"Forget the burn, my dear, let's jerk!"

Its presence makes the day more bright,
In crazy hats, it shines so right.
From kitchen tales to garden charm,
Our agile buddy keeps us warm.

The Green Chronicles.

In a pot so small and stout,
Lives a fiendish plant, no doubt.
With tales of survival quite absurd,
This green buddy's voice is heard.

Each sip of water makes it cheer,
"I'm not a cactus, have no fear!"
With globs of gel for every need,
It thrives on laughter, grows with speed.

When friends come 'round for tea and talk,
This plant's great wit starts to shock.
"Do I look dry? What's wrong with you?
I blossom better with a brew!"

So here's to tales of spiky fun,
Where every leaf brings laughter spun.
With quirks and gags, it steals the show,
My green companion, don't you know?

Beneath the Gentle Succulent

Beneath the leaves, where shadows fall,
There's a friend, who answers all.
With humor packed in every frond,
A quip or two, it loves to respond.

"Water me well," it gives a wink,
"Too much, and I'll likely sink!"
In sunny spots it likes to bask,
With prickly smiles, it's quite the task.

It heals our scrapes with a joyful laugh,
While steering clear of crafty gaffs.
A quirky plant, with vibes so bright,
It lights the room like stars at night.

So let us toast to nature's quirks,
Our green companion, playful works.
In pots of joy, it takes its stand,
A loyal heart, a leafy hand.

Embrace of the Green Companion

Oh, leafy pal, you're quite the joke,
In thriving climes, you love to poke.
With every sprout, you spill your cheer,
A silly plant, I hold you dear.

When summer's heat brings up the sweat,
You know the way to ease the fret.
With gooey charm, you spread the glee,
While laughing at the woes of me.

With friends around, you mingle well,
Beneath your shade, we cast a spell.
A potion here, a prank or two,
Your antics sparkle, ever new.

So here's to you, my spiky mate,
In laughter shared, we celebrate.
With quirky jests and sunny vibes,
Together, we flip the scribe.

Tales from the Terrarium

In a pot of dreams, so bright and green,
Lived a cactus who fancied himself a queen.
He'd prance and he'd preen, quite full of flair,
While the ferns rolled their eyes and tried not to stare.

The snails had a party, with music and cheer,
But the grumpy old moss said, 'You're all too near!'
With a wiggle and jiggle, they slid on the floor,
While the lichen just fumed, 'That's not what I wore!'

A worm passed around some pudding delight,
'Only dessert serves up this much bite!'
The orchids just chuckled, their petals aglow,
In the terrarium's ball, all chaos did flow.

So here's to the plants, with antics galore,
Who dance under the glow of a light from the floor.
In a world full of leaves, with wild, funny scenes,
Who knew that green life could be so routine?

Resilient Bonds

Two succulents grew in a nearby tray,
One stubborn as ox, the other like clay.
'You should try to be wild,' said the prickly old sage,
But the soft one just giggled, 'I prefer my cage!'

They argued and laughed over sunlight and shade,
While a sunbeam of warmth made their worries fade.
'You've got the cool looks,' said the spiky one slow,
'But inside you're as sweet as a marshmallow glow!'

A ladybug came, riding high on a leaf,
Laughed at their banter, then shared her belief.
'It's not how you look, but the fun that you share,
That makes all the green friends too sweet not to care!'

So they swayed in the breeze, bonds resilient and true,
With laughter and banter, their colors did bloom.
Two quirky green pals with nothing to rue,
In a world full of plants, their giggles just grew.

Leaves of Love

In a garden so lush, where the wild vines grow,
A fern told a tale, with a glint and a glow.
'Oh, how I adore the way sunlight does gleam,
Making every leaf sparkle, just like a dream!'

But a petunia scoffed, all pink and quite proud,
'Your flair is for plants, enveloped in cloud!'
'What's wrong with that view?' the fern asked with glee,
'Every petal's a chance for this joy you can see!'

'Love isn't just blooms, it's the laughter we spread,
It's dancing in raindrops, and sweet things we've said.'
With each curl and twist, they spun tales in glee,
Of leaves and their quirks in this vibrant spree.

From sun-kissed to shady, their hearts intertwined,
In a world full of foliage, the best love you'll find.
With roots deep in soil and laughter on high,
These leafy delights were the fun in the sky!

The Geranium's Lament

A geranium sighed with a wobbly stem,
'Why can't I be smooth like that fine tulip gem?'
With petals all crinkled and color in spades,
She fretted and pouted, afraid she'd not fade.

'You're one of a kind!' said a nearby fern,
'Your quirky design makes the garden just turn!
Do not envy the others; embrace what you bear,
Your charm is unique, like a bright, funny flare!'

Ephemeral blooms had their own style and grace,
And though they felt perfect, it's the heart, not the face!
A little laugh rang out, from a bumblebee's wing,
'Life's not just petals, but the joy that you bring!'

So the geranium smiled, and her worries took flight,
In the patch of the garden, everything felt right.
With laughter and love, she'd sway in the breeze,
A quirky old bloom, just delightful with ease!

Spirit of the Succulent

In a pot so bright, she stands tall,
With spiky hair, she won't let you fall.
Sipping sun like it's a tea,
A vibrant life, so carefree.

Her friends all poke, but don't you fret,
They're all sharp, but can't see regret.
A banquet of laughs in this leafy crew,
We plot garden antics, just us two.

She tells silly tales of the rainy days,
How she danced in drops and twirled in rays.
With roots so deep, she knows the fun,
A riotous spirit, a sheen under the sun.

Together we laugh, we'll never get bored,
At least not till our pot gets ignored.
In this green brigade, we won't take life slow,
It's a succulent giggle, a true plant show!

Green Guardians of Serenity

On the windowsill, we stake our ground,
With leaves so sharp and laughter profound.
Guardians bold of the sunny space,
Each day we wear a giggle's grace.

So when the cat walks by in a huff,
We pretend to be tough, but we're really quite fluff.
Our prickly selves can't take it too far,
We're just plant pals, under the same star.

Sharing whispers of sunshine schemes,
Trading care tips and leafy dreams.
We may look fierce, but don't be misled,
Our light-hearted chats are easily fed.

In our green kingdom, fun's never far,
Just a leaf or two, and we'll raise a jar.
Guardians in green, let's raise a toast,
To laughter and growth, we're proud to boast!

Friendship in Flora

In pots aligned on this sunny shelf,
We giggle together, just being ourselves.
She's the sassy one, a queen of the greens,
With a prickly charm that's fit for scenes.

When the new plant arrives, we cast a sly glance,
Making sure they know not to take a chance.
With a spine and a wink, we plot our little games,
But beneath the surface, it's all fun and names.

Water once a week? Oh, what a joke!
We thrive in neglect, a true leaf cloak.
With roots intertwined, we're quite the pair,
In this botanical party, no room for despair.

Our bond is sturdy like a sturdy vine,
Happy to bask in the sun where we shine.
In our leafy realm, fun's here to stay,
With laughter and growth lighting the way!

Whispering Greens

Whispers echo through our leafy domain,
As sunlight dances, we play our game.
With each little poke and gentle tease,
Our days float lightly in the warm breeze.

She brags about her perfect sunbathe,
While I sip on dew, a little less brave.
In this plant pals' realm, every giggle's grand,
As we plot our next move with a leafy hand.

We swap our stories, both wild and quaint,
From battles with bugs to moments of paint.
A green world's wonder with each little chat,
A banquet of fun, just like that!

With roots connecting, we'll stand side by side,
In the laughter of leaves, we'll take our stride.
Whispering dreams in this garden of glee,
Together, forever, just her and me!

www.ingramcontent.com/pod-product-compliance
Lightning Source LLC
Chambersburg PA
CBHW072222070526
44585CB00015B/1448